Six Ways To Enjoy T

Text 60 Minutes	The length of our small books is based on the time in the air of a flight between Toronto and Chicago. Start reading as you take off and finish the book by the time you land. Just the right length for the 21st-century reader.
Cartoons 30 Minutes	You can also gain a complete overview of the ideas in this book by looking at the cartoons and reading the captions. We find the cartoons have made our Strategic Coach concepts accessible to readers as young as eight years old.
Audio 120 Minutes	The audio recording that accompanies this book is not just a recitation of the printed words but an in-depth commentary that expands each chapter's mindset into new dimensions. Download the audio at **strategiccoach.com/go/ah**
Video 30 Minutes	Our video interviews about the concepts in the book deepen your understanding of the mindsets. If you combine text, cartoons, audio, and video, your understanding of the ideas will be 10x greater than you would gain from reading only. Watch the videos at **strategiccoach.com/go/ah**
Scorecard 10 Minutes	Score your American Happiness Mindset at **strategiccoach.com/go/ah**. First, score yourself on where you are now, and then fill in where you want to be a year from now.
ebook 1 Minute	After absorbing the fundamental ideas of the American Happiness concept, you can quickly and easily share them by sending the ebook version to as many other individuals as you desire. Direct them to **strategiccoach.com/go/ah**

Foreword

I'm delighted to introduce you to this powerful little book that uniquely explains why *happy* Americans right now are so different from all those who say they are unhappy.

For the past three years, I've partnered with Dan Sullivan in our regular podcast series, "The American Checklist." Over many dozens of episodes, we've explored the eight crucial mindsets that, when combined and strengthened over a lifetime, make Americans the happiest individuals on the planet. Indeed, they are the happiest individuals who have ever lived.

The many hours of creative discussion with Dan have greatly simplified my own understanding of how I can further increase my personal American happiness. Our joint exploration has given me a startling new and simple way of understanding where so many unhappy Americans are missing the mark in the current period.

American Happiness is a creative process that defines an ever-expanding collaboration that is possible between a uniquely designed country and every freedom-minded individual in today's world who decides to take advantage of the opportunity.

At the very center of American Happiness, going back more than two centuries, is an extraordinary "double bet." The Founding Fathers bet the entire future of the new country on countless unpredictable individuals betting uniquely on their own futures.

Going back to the 1700s, Americans, attracted from all over the world, understood this double bet and have continually created their own happiness. Right now, underneath the seeming complications, confusion, and conflicts that fill daily news commentary, the double bet formula is more available to committed and courageous individuals than ever before.

Dan Sullivan and I intend this book to be read, discussed, and shared by everyone who is betting on their American future.

Each of the eight mindsets covered in the following chapters is energizing in itself—and exponentially productive when combined with the other seven mindsets into a growing lifetime capability.

By mastering the American Happiness mindsets, day by day, you will find yourself increasingly immune to the antics and attacks of unhappy individuals who never understood the extraordinary double bet that is growing all around them.

You will always be creating your own happiness and expanding it to others.

Mark Young

Cartoons by Hamish MacDonald.

Printed in Toronto, Canada. The Strategic Coach Inc., 33 Fraser Avenue, Suite 201, Toronto, Ontario, M6K 3J9.

This publication is meant to strengthen your common sense, not to substitute for it. It is also not a substitute for the advice of your doctor, lawyer, accountant, or any of your advisors, personal or professional.

If you would like further information about The Strategic Coach® Program or other Strategic Coach® services and products, please telephone 416.531.7399 or 1.800.387.3206.

Library and Archives Canada Cataloguing in Publication

Title: American happiness / Dan Sullivan.
Names: Sullivan, Dan, 1944- author.
Identifiers: Canadiana 20210323248 | ISBN 9781897239773 (softcover)
Subjects: LCSH: Happiness—United States. | LCSH: Self-realization—United States.
Classification: LCC BF575.H27 S85 2021 | DDC 152.4/2—dc23

Contents

Introduction

Pursuit Of Happiness

You realize that being an American comes, first of all, from the goal of making your life about achieving individual happiness. And anyone can do this.

The distinctly American emphasis on the individual's pursuit of happiness makes all the difference in how Americans think about and live their lives in the 21st century.

Simply put, the United States was the first country on the planet that was consciously invented for the purpose of "pursuing happiness." It says so right in the founding document. Americans were committed to a place where happiness was something everyone could pursue.

American society protects your life and gives you liberty so that you, as an individual, can pursue happiness. It's a remarkable formula, and this is the only country where this is the mission statement.

I've identified eight mindsets that make someone a happy American, and in the following chapters, I'll explore each one. The eight mindsets are *individualism, ingenuity, exceptionalism, teamwork, growth, transformation, winning,* and *transcendence*.

"Happy" as a lifetime goal.

For those who possess these mindsets, it doesn't matter how their life started or where they came from. The most important thing to them is where they're going and how they're going to get there. No matter what they've been told to think about by other people, the most important goal they'll ever have is living a life that makes them happy.

What makes for happiness is something you have to figure out for yourself because it's different for every person on the planet. And you're free to figure out what you personally need in order to be happy.

Like all individuals, you're responsible for finding your own happiness, but you're not responsible for anyone else's happiness. The U.S. is the country it is because of its formula for individual happiness: each individual pursuing their own happiness means that things work out well for the country.

Only individuals can do this.

You are your biggest and most important responsibility, and no one else is responsible for you and your life. There are people who have helped you and cared for you. There are people whom you care for and love. But only you are responsible for the life you'll always be creating.

No one knows how any individual's life is going to turn out. It's always a mystery. But each person is given as much freedom as possible, and they can determine how they want to proceed.

This is the bet that the United States makes. The Founders bet that a large percentage of individuals, if given the freedom to pursue their own happiness, will choose to do things that are good for them. And as a result of doing good things for themselves, they'll also produce improvements and progress that benefit everyone else.

They bet that the expansion of the eight happiness mindsets among millions of individuals will continually transform the growing security, success, and prosperity of the American nation—in unpredictable ways.

Creating something new.

You were born with unique capabilities, and you continually experience unique challenges that you have to transform. By using your abilities to transform your challenges, you can create entirely new opportunities that lead to entirely new achievements and results.

This movement toward the creation of something new was part of America even before the revolution took place. Each of the colonies was like a new country, but they knew they'd only be safe if all the individual colonies united as one country because they needed much greater societal depth and power.

The only way to start something new was with a formula that had never existed before. And the formula was simple: *We're going to bet the future of the country on unpredictable individuals betting on themselves.*

Never done before now.

Your future is completely open and unpredictable. Regardless of what other people had achieved before you arrived, you're as free to create your own exceptional future as you choose to be. Your future impact, value, and meaning can be as exceptional as you make them.

You have life and liberty, and you're free to pursue your own happiness. This means you have to give up blaming others for anything that happened in the past. And to the degree that you give up blame for the past, you have the freedom to take advantage of the future. It's a decisive moment in human history where individuals are given the right to choose the future. And in order to do that, all they have to give up is blame and condemnation of the past. But they must make this choice.

Combining unique skills.

You have a secret American power that will always multiply you as an individual: you can continually combine your unique ambition and capabilities with those of an increasing number of others to create extraordinary teamwork in every area of life that interests you.

You have the right to pursue your own happiness. This means that you have to accept that everyone else also has that same right.

And your pursuit of happiness is unique. You're going to go about pursuing your happiness in one way, and every other individual is going to do it in their own way. Every person has their own unique goals, knowledge, and skills. And if two people combine their uniqueness, they're going to come up with something much bigger than either individual could have achieved on their own.

You have the opportunity to do this, but success isn't guaranteed. You have to put in the work, you have to be smart, and you have to know how to cooperate.

The American experience is unique in the world, putting an emphasis on freedom and happiness. But to truly take advantage of this, you need to adopt and develop eight mindsets that will set you up for success.

UNIQUE START...
BETTING THE COUNTRY...
HOW ABOUT "PURSUIT OF HAPPINESS"?
1700
1750
1800
1850

...EXTRAORDINARY GROWTH
...BETTING ON YOURSELF
1900
1950
2000
2050

Chapter 1
Individualism

You focus on expanding your own capabilities, resources, and opportunities regardless of what others may think about this.

Sometime in the past, you had a fundamental breakthrough. You probably remember where and when this breakthrough happened. At some point, *you made a lifetime bet on yourself*. In other words, you made the decision to relieve everyone else of the responsibility for making your life a success, for making your life easier, and for making your life satisfying and meaningful.

And you also realized that you're not responsible for ensuring any of these results for anyone else.

Americans are happy when they bet on themselves. And being American means you're freed up to be able to bet on yourself. The United States is depending on this. It has faith that if a large number of its citizens bet on themselves, then overall circumstances will improve as a result.

And when someone bets on themselves, it's impossible for anyone else to predict how it will go.

Fundamental building block.

You feel fortunate to be an American because the U.S. is the only country that was designed from the start with individualism as its fundamental foundation. You know that if you choose to develop yourself as an increasingly more successful individual, the country will support your choice.

The freedom for individuals to develop themselves is part of the American structure. It's built into the walls and the furniture. It's the electricity that runs it. The mindset has been passed from generation to generation for 400 years, so it has a lot of momentum!

This building block of individualism is one of the reasons why many people from around the world immigrate to the U.S. But if you have a mindset that's contrary to it, whether you're born in the U.S. or not, you won't find support there.

Protecting individual freedom.

You know that the phrase "life, liberty, and the pursuit of happiness" is all about your freedom to be as successful as you want to be as an individual. This is what all the structures and processes of the country are constituted to protect. America protects your right to be who you want to be.

Freedom for one person to develop themselves in the way they want means freedom for everyone to do the same. Because of this, when you notice that another individual's freedom is being threatened, you'll want to defend it. You're fighting for your own freedom as well as for everyone else's. You're not fighting for "the nation" or for any abstraction. The fight for each individual's freedom is one you can personalize. You're fighting for your neighbor's freedom because your own freedom is only as good as theirs.

Encouraging individual talent.

America encourages you to be as successfully talented as possible. You can focus for your whole life on the unique talents you were born with. But it's your responsibility to discover what your talents are, and it's your lifetime project to utilize your talents in ways that are valuable and useful to others.

Your talents are only truly useful if someone else thinks they're useful and is willing to pay for your talents, go out of their way to encourage your talents, and recommend your talents. Your talents have no use if you're isolated. They're useful to the degree that other people find them useful.

People experience real pleasure when they're suddenly surprised by a new talent they hadn't encountered before because it opens up their sense of what's possible.

Suddenly, a skilled person with a new idea who's devoted their life to developing this skill emerges, and it makes people very hopeful about the future. They know that new, surprising things will happen in unpredictable ways. Americans know that what's possible in their future is always bigger and more exciting than anything that happened in the past.

Rewarding individual achievement.

In the U.S., you won't run out of ways in which you can be individually successful. There are almost endless kinds of individual achievements that can be richly rewarded, with new possibilities continually being created.

Individual achievement doesn't get rewarded in general terms—it gets rewarded by other unique individuals who are excited about what you're doing.

The American mindsets we're discussing here—*individualism, ingenuity, exceptionalism, teamwork, growth, transformation, winning,* and *transcendence*—give you the chance to be continually rewarded, but you have to keep growing. If you stop growing, you'll stop being excited by other people's success and start becoming bothered by it.

Once you're no longer growing, you're no longer interesting. People who are taking action and always improving are the only players that really matter in the U.S. In certain other countries and regimes, the emphasis is on maintaining the status quo. But in America, the spotlight is on those who create unique value as individuals.

Trusting in unpredictable cooperation.
Since the beginning, American society has been decentralized. After all, it can't be centralized if you're betting on unpredictable individuals.

And ambitious Americans, as individuals, create unique ways to cooperate with one another. In this way, each individual's uniqueness gets increasingly multiplied by the uniqueness of many other ambitious individuals.

All of this combining and multiplying is always unpredictable. In fact, what gives you ever-greater opportunity is that it's unpredictable and there are no guarantees. So you have to be okay with unpredictability and see it as an advantage.

This game was designed to be played over the long term. You don't worry about a time when you'll run out of talent or ideas. The country is betting on you continually using your uniqueness to create value, and it's going to support you in all your efforts to do so.

And Americans who freely bet on themselves in unpredictable ways will increasingly develop and enjoy the eight "American Happiness" mindsets.

EVERYTHING STARTS...
OPPORTUNITY
OPPORTUNITY
RESOURCES
RESOURCES

...WITH INDIVIDUALS
RESOURCES
RESOURCES
CAPABILITY
CAPABILITY
CAPABILITY
PI
sS

Chapter 2
Ingenuity
You're committed to creating new ways of achieving uniquely new and better results in every area of your life for yourself and others.

In America, enormous value is placed on individuals who create new ways of doing things that improve the lives of others. And this is what entrepreneurs do. You use your brain to take something that exists and make it more useful and valuable. And this starts with individuality, the mindset discussed in the previous chapter, because without it, you'd never think of doing things differently than the people who came before you.

You always have your own ideas about the best ways to get things done in every area of your life. Sometimes, these are entirely new inventions, and sometimes, they're small, incremental improvements.

You're someone whom others look to for many kinds of problem solving. You're good to have around in any area of activity because you look at everything with new eyes. You think about how things can work in new and different ways. Having you around makes everyone more confident that things are going to get better—what's broken will be fixed, and old, faulty methods will be replaced by new, efficient ways of doing things. When you come around, everyone feels more energetic and optimistic because something surprising and clever is about to be created.

Not like everyone else.

Your inventiveness is a treat for everyone because it means things can always change for the better in totally surprising ways. You put ordinary things together in extraordinary new systems that produce unexpected results. Where others might complain about an obstacle, you smoothly create a way around it.

When the first settlers came to the Americas, it was a big risk to take that ocean voyage from European countries to an entirely unknown continent. It attracted the most individualistic people, and in order to survive, they also had to be ingenious.

In a collectivist society, you have to be like everyone else in order to reinforce the collective identity. But the new system created by the settlers bet on every individual not being like everyone else. It's not that it's expected that you won't get along with others; it's that you'll feel the personal confidence and get the personal reward of arranging your own life differently and trying out new things. And if you find something that works for you, the bet is that you'll want to share it with others in exchange for valuable things they've created that are different from yours. So, uniquely different individuals are always benefiting from one another.

Magic-like problem solving.

As an entrepreneur, you've spent your life learning how to solve problems that others can't comprehend. Where it's all complexity and confusion for them, it's clear, simple, and easy for you. It's your greatest pleasure helping others out, and to them, your solutions seem like magic.

Equality doesn't enter into this. Some people are uniquely gifted at it, and others less so.

Since everybody's allowed to experiment with their life, there are many different things you could focus on to improve. If you're focusing on one thing, you're not focusing on others, but other people are choosing to focus on those.

In the U.S., you're encouraged to focus on different things to see what you come up with because that will make you happier, but also because different individuals focusing on making improvements in a wide variety of areas is beneficial for everyone.

Creating something new.

You were born with unique capabilities, and you continually experience unique challenges that need to be transformed. By using your abilities to transform your challenges, you can create entirely new opportunities that lead to entirely new achievements and results.

Instead of being punished for your uniqueness, you're encouraged. And if what you produce is useful and valuable, you're rewarded and praised for it.

That a society should form itself with the objectives of ingenuity and transformation in mind is unique. This isn't for everybody, but those who made the trip created a fresh start, with a new set of mindsets.

Focus on what's not working.

Almost everything can be improved, not just once, but continually. It's an easy thing to do once you can imagine what the better version looks like. And you know it's never about the invention itself, but how everyone is going to benefit after you pull it off.

There's so much opportunity all around, and by focusing on what's not working—surveying what's around you, homing in on things that you don't like, and figuring out how to improve them—you develop a sense that everything that exists can be improved.

And in America, you have not only full permission to go about things in this way, but encouragement.

Questioning is the key.

In the realm of thinking, there are two main territories: the territory of answers, and the territory of questions. Collectives are created in the territory of answers, and the American experiment was created in the territory of questions:

Why do we do it this way? Where did that come from? Who thought this was a good idea? What's changed that calls for something new?

You love asking questions that get everybody else thinking new thoughts. New questions create new possibilities that lead to new experiments and to new, better solutions.

Since I was the fifth child born in my family, everything about the family operation was already set by the time I came around. At an early age, I discovered that by asking questions, I could learn what people wanted and then figure out where I fit in and what I could contribute. And what became a governing question for me that continues to this day is, "How far can I go?"

When people free up their ability to question, anything is possible.

ALWAYS IMPROVING...
$$ + X
=
$$$$
ALW
GET
BET

...UNIQUE BREAKTHROUGHS
AYS
TING
TER

Chapter 3

Exceptionalism

You're always differentiating yourself and those you cooperate with as uniquely better than everyone else.

Your growing ingenuity as a confident individual enables you to create new kinds of value in your everyday work and life, and your increasing knowledge and capabilities are focused more and more on exceptional performance and results.

No one can predict what will be created or who will do it, but America bets that if it gives total encouragement for people to be ingenious, some individuals will create innovations that will benefit everyone.

Over the course of your life, you develop your own approaches to learning and achieving that are tested by practical success and failure. Throughout this process, you understand that you have to utilize what you're best at and most love doing to create some value outside of yourself that others are willing to support and pay for. And you appreciate that everyone else also has unique capabilities, different from yours, that can be exceptional.

Measuring against yourself.

You can't be the only one striving for exceptional feats because the system is set up so that everyone has the same opportunities. And to be a happy American, you have to be happy with how the system is set up.

But one of the conditions of individualism is that you can't measure what you're doing against what others are doing. Each person is different, and they're doing something different with what makes them different. Concepts like *better* or *worse* don't apply here, and you can't measure your own progress against someone else's.

The only proper measurement for what you're doing is how far you've come from where you started.

You've always had the sense that you're you and not someone else—you've had a unique sense of self. And you're always learning from others because your own experience is your lifetime teacher. From the very start, you've measured your progress by who you used to be to see how much you've changed and grown. This makes you uniquely capable and confidently different.

Different plan and path.

You continually make up your own rules for creating your future progress and enjoyment. From an early age, you viewed what other people were doing as interesting, educational, and entertaining, but not what's most important to you. You can learn from what other people are doing with their own individualism and ingenuity, but it doesn't have to dictate what you'll do. Being independent in both thinking and action always tells you what's next.

As an American, you're encouraged and supported to be unique and to take your uniqueness as far as you want to. You have to create your own path and make your own plan for achieving your goals. You can take advantage of what others have created, using their paths and plans, but you don't have to conform. You're given encouragement, but you have to choose and create your own direction. You're not given directions that you must obey.

Understanding others' perspectives.

You have an inborn sense of fairness about life beyond yourself. You recognize that everything you want for yourself is only possible if others can enjoy the same opportunities and advantages. Indeed, you have an unusual, growing ability to see things from others' points of view.

A key part of the American experiment is that all of the support and opportunities you're granted as an individual are also granted to everyone else. There's no reason to take someone else's success personally—they're not in competition with you.

Each individual's success exists in areas that they're creating, which means that space for success isn't limited. No one's success is going to get in the way of yours. There's no end to the space that's going to be available for you to be who you want to be.

Also, it benefits you to pay attention to what other people are doing with their unique individualism, which is different from what you're doing with yours, as you might benefit from their innovations and might even be able to contribute to them through collaboration.

Value creation reality.

You're continually visualizing new, bigger, and better ways to achieve progress with your exceptional skills. You measure your growth by the increasing positive impact you're making on the world around you, and your growing impact enables an expanding number of people to improve their lives.

So it's not just about the progress you've made as an individual. It's about how you use your individual uniqueness to make things better and easier for other people in brand new ways.

The feedback you get from doing this will be clear, and you'll know when you have to make changes to what you're doing in order to make the positive impact you want to have.

Attracting exceptional cooperation.

Your exceptional performance, results, and rewards increasingly attract the interest of other like-minded individuals who have exceptional capabilities that support and encourage yours. You use one another's ingenuity to create even bigger and better opportunities that attract still others. It's a self-modifying system, continually providing the fuel to propel itself.

You have your own lane, and you have no say in where everyone else's lanes take them. You appreciate that they're out there, and you always have an eye out for people who are headed in the same direction as you are.

Those other individuals, who have the same mindsets as you do, are the people you want to collaborate with. Your exceptionalism combined with their exceptionalism results in both of you doing bigger and better exceptional things together. That's the expansive formula.

UNIQUELY DIFFERENT
MEASURING PROGRESS
HOW DO I JOIN?
OWN PLAN AND PATH
WHO SAID YOU COULD DO THIS?
NO ONE!
UNDERSTANDING OTHERS

UNIQUELY USEFUL
I JUST WANT TO BLEND IN!
ATTRACTING COOPERATION
WHERE ARE THE RULES?!
VALUE CREATION

Chapter 4

Teamwork

You're continually increasing your collaboration with other talented and successful achievers to create new kinds of value.

The U.S. puts an enormous emphasis on individualism. But it isn't lonely individualism—it's *cooperative* individualism. The breakthroughs the U.S. has made and continues to make as a society have come about because of creative teams made up of very powerful individuals who lend their skills to other people's skills. And it's not an addition process, but a multiplication process.

Your deepening clarity about your own unique ambition, capabilities, and opportunities continually expands your successful cooperation with others. The combined focus, performance, and impact of the teamwork always produces breakthroughs that none of you could have achieved on your own. Your unique teamwork contributions multiply what others can achieve. And everyone else's energy and support multiply your confidence to contribute even more.

Greater collaboration.

As your experience of successful teamwork expands, you keep entering into creative collaboration with more capable and confident individuals.

Americans' lasting, impactful breakthroughs are not created by individuals going about it alone. Even when an achievement seems from the outside to be a solo performance, there's likely a team of skilled individuals enabling that performance to occur.

Saving time and energy.

You always see your own knowledge and skills as resources that can be multiplied through endless teamwork. You're increasingly focused on saving your time and energy by combining what you're uniquely good at with the different capabilities of other like-minded individuals.

Alone, you'd be doing everything yourself. On a team, you're doing only what you're great at, and the rest of the work is being handled by people who are great at those activities.

There's no envy, competition, or self-comparison on a great team because everybody else's skills are needed for you to improve. You contribute what you're uniquely great at to other people who are uniquely great at other things, and that's how you multiply your capabilities. Everybody gains, and nobody loses.

Focused and purposeful.

You continually choose bigger and better teamwork possibilities, while at the same time deepening and expanding your impact inside of each new experience. More and more, you focus on where your skills are uniquely valuable to others, while including others' unique capabilities in your own bigger projects.

Teams have leaders, and the leader's unique capability is to envision a purpose and to articulate that purpose to a team of other individuals. The leader's main role is to energize the unique capabilities of every other collaborator on the team in order for the entire team to reach their shared goal.

This is what talented, capable people are looking for. And if they're not getting that focus, purpose, and leadership, they'll head elsewhere.

Teamwork breakthroughs.

You make your best progress within big teamwork achievements, and this is where you're uniquely useful. Everyone on the team is motivated and focused. The goals are always accessible, achievable, and measurable. Everyone, including you, contributes what they do best and what they most love doing.

Every time a team creates a breakthrough in a new area, there are actually two breakthroughs taking place. The first is that the bigger, better, measurable goal has been achieved, and the second is the new form of teamwork that's been created, which is something that can be captured and repeated.

And each time you use the teamwork breakthrough formula that you created, you discover more and more ways to make the process more effective and fun. You'll figure out standards that you always make sure to reach, and these will ensure that the work of the entire team is as efficient as it can be.

You multiply them.

You always feel proudest of using your best skills to multiply other people's best talents. You attract other ingenious individuals into your best projects, giving them a powerful purpose for their best efforts and results. This is enormously satisfying and motivating for them and for you.

At every level of your growth, you're looking for people to work with who are going to pull you to a higher level. And guess what—that's why they're choosing to work with you too. They feel that if they work with you, you'll multiply them.

You're not competing with them in the area they're great at. They're freed up by the rest of the team to be great at what they do. Everybody on the team being uniquely great motivates everybody else on the team to be uniquely great.

This is something you never need to communicate in words. The teamwork itself, and the higher levels of performance, sends the message.

They multiply you.

You'll discover that the more you help other team members make progress, the more committed they'll be to doing the same for you. New possibilities for improvement emerge, and new kinds of breakthroughs occur. The more that your creativity and skills expand your team members' futures, the more that your future is multiplied by theirs. It's all reciprocal.

The U.S. is the first country in the world to bet its future on unpredictable individuals. But the only time this is a good bet is when the individuals bet on themselves and create progress for everybody else. And if those people engage in teamwork with one another, the progress multiplies.

It's always unpredictable who will bet on themselves, but they're the people who will create the greatest lasting improvements.

YOU MULTIPLY THEM
TIME

THEY MULTIPLY YOU
US
TEAMWORK
TEAMWORK
PURPOSE

Chapter 5

Growth

You're always improving every area of your life in ways that are increasingly measurable and satisfying.

When you envision your future, it's always bigger and better than where you are now. That's because where you are currently always surpasses where you started from in every area of performance and results. You're always growing, and as a result, everything and everyone around you is always growing. As soon as you complete each new growth achievement, you can immediately see where the next achievement can begin.

You'll always be growing, and there's never a future point where you see yourself stopping. When others feel that they've grown enough and are slowing down, you'll be passing them and speeding up. Wherever you are, everything grows.

The U.S. is betting on individuals who won't just stop someday. And you recognize that retirement isn't a reward, as many people think it is. Retirement means being taken out of use, which is not one of your goals. Your goal is to always be useful and always be growing.

Always bigger, always better.

You enjoy where you are, regardless of where you are, because you're always improving everything you encounter. Whatever you have, you always work to have more of it. And everything you make bigger is always better. It's always more satisfying and meaningful, and it motivates you to grow even more.

Like all the mindsets discussed in this book, the growth mindset is also held by many people in other countries. This is the reason why so many creative individuals want to come to the U.S.

They live in countries that don't bet on individuals to create and grow, so they want to come to the country that does exactly that. And in the U.S., from the founding of the country, there has never been a limit on how much growth is desired or encouraged.

Every area of your life.

You notice that many other people are trying to get away from where they are, always trying to be somewhere they're not. But that's not you. You take what's available and make it more useful and meaningful, and this increasing improvement is happening in every area of your work life and personal life.

There's room in the U.S. for people who don't want to be individuals and who are unexceptional and unskilled at teamwork. They will be provided for by the system, but they won't be happy Americans.

Happy Americans are ones who hold these mindsets. Knowing this and seeing the example of happy Americans, unhappy Americans can be inspired to make changes in their own mindsets so they can achieve some of that happiness for themselves.

Growing performance.

You measure your growth and performance by big and small

jumps in what you can do now that you couldn't do in the past. What you're able to achieve today is greater than what you could do yesterday. You know that your results next week, next quarter, and next year will always demonstrate greater skill than you have now.

Your performance has nothing to do with self-esteem. Self-esteem is a game you play by yourself, and it has nothing to do with ingenuity or creating value for other people. Performing well in business is how creative, collaborative people make great contributions. And so, you measure the growth in your performance not only by achievement, but by its impact on others. You gain investment and support from the outside, and your confidence grows.

Growing results.

You're always producing and achieving higher levels of results both on your own and through teamwork with others. You're always growing as someone who is useful and valuable to have around. People who are passionate about breakthrough results want your usefulness in the center.

But your growth is not a ceaseless, continuous process. It's a series of jumps to higher levels. Performance and results go together. You take on new projects, experience new achievements, and your performance grows. And part of the reason why your performance grows is that you only have to achieve something that's measurable in the near future. You take breaks and then you're back at it. But the next game is the bigger game. And it's measured by the results of your performance.

This is the opposite of what happens in bureaucracy.

Nothing that happens within bureaucracy makes people happy. In fact, bureaucracy is a way of keeping unhappy Americans organized.

Accelerating, never-ending growth.

Your goal is to be growing on the day you die. Put simply, no slowing down and no stopping, other than breaks before taking bigger jumps. Retirement is never even a thought in your mind. Another 10 years, 25, maybe even 50, you keep growing as others are quitting.

I don't know when I'm going to die, but I know that on that day, I'll be growing. Retirement is the narrative that most people go by, but entrepreneurs don't have to subscribe to that. You can and you must eliminate all alternatives from your future except to always be growing.

If you work for a big corporation, it's impossible to predict your future. You wonder if you're going to be employed, if the company you currently work for is going to continue to exist, and if what you're spending your time doing is even useful.

Entrepreneurs don't have to wonder about those things. In this respect, it's much simpler to be an entrepreneur. Being a happy American is much easier than being an unhappy American because the system was set up for you. Just stick to the eight mindsets and let them reinforce one another.

You might not be running the same organization you are now in 25 years, but you know you're going to be working on something you created and that you'll always be creating greater and greater value for other people.

ALWAYS BIGGER

ALWAYS BETTER

Chapter 6
Transformation

You're always changing your circumstances by first changing yourself, which encourages others to follow your example.

Throughout your life, day by day, year by year, you continually encounter situations and circumstances that don't meet your growth standards, and you immediately feel compelled to improve them. This always starts by transforming your internal mindsets, commitments, and courage, which immediately transforms your individual capability and confidence to make things better. And the more you do this, taking responsibility for improving things starting with yourself, the easier it becomes to do.

Over and over, you keep becoming a more powerful and successful transformer. It starts by thinking about things differently, which naturally impacts the actions you take, the plans you make, how you communicate with others, and how you organize things around you.

It's actually your decision to transform how you experience something that transforms the experience. You don't have the power to change everything, but you do have the power to change yourself.

Very quickly, after you've become a more skillful transformer on your own, your always improving performance develops into many kinds of teamwork. Your transformative impact keeps expanding out into the world.

Situations and circumstances.

You're always making things bigger and better wherever you go. You continually improve every situation and transform every circumstance. Everything gets more abundant and enjoyable as a result of your transformative mindsets and capabilities. You leave everything better than you found it.

If you think about all the people you've admired most, you'll discover that each one of those individuals was transformational. A person can be talented, smart, and clever, but all of those characteristics fade if they don't use them to make a unique mark. Yet, we always remember transformational people.

And the biggest transformation that is honored in the United States is when a single individual has the impact of making others' lives better.

Improving what you don't like.

Every person in the world has things they like and don't like. This is how we discover our uniqueness. Uniqueness is the clash between liking and disliking that moves us to create something new.

And it's no one's responsibility to make your life to your liking. Parents can arrange it so that a child's circumstances are positive, but it's ultimately up to each individual to take responsibility for fashioning their own life to their liking. The world wasn't created for you, and it's up to you to make the changes you want, according to your unique likes and dislikes.

As you keep achieving results at higher levels, you become crystal clear about what you like and what you don't like. When you encounter situations that you find deficient, you transform the conditions into something bigger and better.

When you encounter negative circumstances, you transform them into exceptional and lasting positives.

And you focus on things that are a big deal for you, not bothering with things that aren't.

Internal transformation first.

Growing your ability to transform the world outside of you always starts by improving yourself on the inside. You heighten your mindsets, focus your commitments, and muster greater courage. Every time you do this internally, you immediately and automatically become a more powerful transformer externally.

Unlike other countries, the U.S. is a place where if you continually choose to transform yourself internally, it generally gets rewarded, and oftentimes, it gets rewarded very quickly. In other words, if you make yourself into a better person, you'll be rewarded for it.

The country bets on individuals betting on themselves, and betting on yourself is what you're doing when you choose to transform yourself internally in order to change your external circumstances.

Always more skillful individual.

A fundamental part of your happiness is knowing you're in a country that's betting on you to bet on yourself. And you can get continually more skillful at betting on yourself in a country that bets on you.

Those who admire you are especially impressed with your never-ending improvement of your daily performance and results. You're always getting better. Your contribution to everything you're involved in keeps growing in value. With you along, everyone else feels increasingly more capable and confident.

We get to choose who we're influenced by and who we're an influence on, and being transformational is the common ground. You want to be influenced by transformational people, and you want to be a transformational person for others who can benefit from your influence.

Expanding teamwork transformation.

The best way to attract great teamwork is to work on yourself. This means you put in the work individually so that you become someone whom other great people would want to be in teamwork with. Indeed, great teams are made up of people who improve themselves so that they can be of greater benefit to the other members of the team.

When you focus on transforming things in your life for the better, you invite other transformation-minded individuals to join you as members of great teams. As your teams grow more successful at turning negatives into positives, other transformative teams collaborate with yours.

This is self-perpetuating. Transformation-minded people are always finding bigger, better things to work on, creating greater value. Otherwise, they get bored.

And transformational people don't dwell on the negative—they see where there's new opportunity to create something positive. While other people complain about the past, you put things together in a new way in order to produce better results in the future.

CHANGING YOUR CIRCUMSTANCES...
BIGGER
AND
BETTER
FLOUR
FLOUR
FLOUR
EXPANDING TEAMWORK

...BY CHANGING YOURSELF
ALWAYS IMPROVING
FROM THE INSIDE OUT
GROWING SKILL
GROWING VALUE
1
100
1,000

Chapter 7

Winning

You love coming out on top and coming out ahead in entirely new ways, and this inspires others to strive in the same way.

You're always motivated to achieve bigger and better things in entirely new ways. That's what "winning" means to you, and because you're always improving as an ingenious individual, and always expanding your teamwork in every area of your life, winning is an endless possibility.

You notice that winning is an activity that continually generates its own new goals and motivation. Win once, and you automatically want to do it again. In fact, winning means you can make an even bigger bet next time.

Both winning and losing can be intensely emotional experiences. In the U.S., when someone loses and accepts losing as being their future, they're out of the game.

What you do, on the other hand, is continually push your capabilities and results further, and the difference between where you were before and the new standard you've set is the realm of winning. You're always winning in new ways, because winning in old ways isn't interesting to you, and there's no transformation in that.

You're always aiming to reach higher than you ever have before, always going further than where you are now.

Endless ways to win.

You've grasped that America's bet on unpredictable individuals means new ways of winning are always ingeniously proliferating and that you can continually be creating new ways of surpassing your past achievements and successes. You're always doing this both on your own and through expanding teamwork.

In the U.S. marketplace, the pricing mechanism tells you whether what you're doing is a win or a loss. What people are willing to pay you for your offering is the measurement of your success. There's no reward for losing, and you're not going to move from a loss to a win if you don't learn from the experience of losing.

Failure is only failure if you stop there, but if you learn from losing, you'll keep finding new ways of winning. You only lose if you give up the game. Staying in the game is where the reward is.

Winning generates goals.

Winning is a powerful, clear-cut, motivating goal. Every time you achieve a win in one area of your life, it's immediately easier to establish a bigger win as a more meaningful goal in another. And all of your winning achievements generate even greater momentum when you're transforming negatives into positives.

If you're playing the game, every time you do something, it has to be better than you did it the time before. You use specific, measurable, actionable goals to make sure that every win is greater than the previous one. At the outset of each project, you're looking at how you can achieve faster, easier, cheaper, and bigger results. And the verdict comes from outside—from check-writers.

You're always working harder than before, you're always setting bigger goals than before, and all this means that you're never going to get tired of playing the game and winning at it.

Ingenuity times teamwork.

Thinking of your next most ambitious goal as a winning objective enables you to tap directly into your two most powerful resources: your own ingenuity and your best available teamwork with other ingenious individuals. This isn't just doubling a winning formula—it can easily lead to a 10x greater result.

You have an idea about how to win, and you have a system for winning. So if you take the idea and the system and put them together, your results will be exponentially bigger.

The more individuals you have on your team multiplying their capabilities toward a new strategy, the bigger the win you'll create. It's your team, so you decide whom you want on it, and it's a better bet when all team members are self-transforming winners.

Surrounded by winners.

If you want to be a winner, don't surround yourself with losers. Losers are people who have given up and stopped playing the game.

The more committed and capable individuals you invite into your teamwork achievements, the more you'll feel surrounded and supported by winners. Working with proven winners means you can make bigger bets on what you can achieve.

Winning for everyone is a clear measurement for having increased both individual capability and confidence within an expanding structure of creative cooperation.

And being a winner means that every bet you make on yourself is bigger than the last one, and every achievement is greater than the previous. In this way, you keep redefining what winning is.

Aiming higher, going further.

As an entrepreneur, you can continue playing the game as long as you like. No person or system can dictate that you have to stop playing at a certain point. Ending the game is strictly self-imposed, and if you don't see an end to your entrepreneurship, then all sorts of things become possible.

Nothing from the outside can prevent you from playing, so you'll continue pulling off winning achievements because the game comes from inside of you.

When someone operates on their own with goals that they keep to themselves, there is an inevitable point where winning is no longer meaningful. But your goal of winning as a unique individual within a winning team continually introduces new ways of surpassing all of your past achievements and successes.

Operating entirely on your own is like playing chess against yourself. It might be interesting for a little while, but there's no risk and no possibility of something new. With a winning team, the team keeps bringing in new capabilities, new ideas, and new strategies. Your own capability keeps growing, and so does the capability around you, and that's always unpredictable.

BIGGER FUTURE...
WINNING
WINNING
WINNING
YOU GO!
YES!

...BIGGER RESULTS
WIN!
ALMOST THERE
WINNING
WINNING
YAY!

Chapter 8

Transcendence

Your sense of a personal lifetime partnership with God always gives you greater confidence, capability, and purpose.

You always have the feeling of connection with a source of power that is greater than anyone can explain. This connectedness is at the center of your sense of being a unique individual. It transcends everything else that you think about your life.

Being transcendently connected and supported is a constant, daily experience and has been for as long as you can remember. It's not a belief that you have to defend. It's not something that you need to argue about or prove. This transcendent confidence is uniquely yours regardless of whether anyone else believes in it.

This belief isn't particular to any religious following. There are big differences between different religions and their practices, but the way that each happy American sees their relationship with a higher power is very similar. It's a uniquely individualistic take on religion, not seeing any intermediaries between you and God, and you don't even have to subscribe to a religion to have that relationship.

There from the beginning.

Your unique, individual experience of being connected to a higher power is something that's been with you from an early age. In fact, it's been with you for as long as you've realized that you were *you*. That is when you realized that you could feel different feelings and think different thoughts than other individuals.

I've always had the sense that there's a divine intelligence and that this intelligence likes me and gives me a lot of approval and support. But my learning is my own, and when I make a mistake or things don't go my way, it's never because God is angry with me. It's not that type of relationship; it's a benevolent one.

And I believe that when you help people see their uniqueness and combine that uniqueness with other people's to create greater value, you're doing God's work.

Never feeling alone.

Your lifetime experience of a transcendent relationship means you always feel connected. Regardless of where you are or what you're doing, you never feel excluded or isolated. Confident of your higher relationship, you're always deepening and expanding your American happiness mindsets.

I've never felt like I was alone, and wherever I am, I feel like I'm at home.

Most people don't operate this way, but I'm far from alone in it. Based on my experience, I can very quickly spot people who also experience life in this way. These are the people who are confident in their feelings of belonging and who are completely at ease with their existence.

You can also easily recognize the opposite—people who are isolated from others. There's a real danger in people being isolated. They lose confidence very quickly, and when people aren't operating from confidence, they think, communicate, and act in ways that don't serve them well. Isolated humans are not good for themselves or other people. It's important to get them connected.

Your proof is your growth.

Your lifetime experience of being in a connected and cooperative partnership with a higher power means that you grow independently as a uniquely ingenious individual. You measure yourself and your progress by an outside standard for growth that is not based on other people's performance or results.

You are completely lacking a sense of entitlement, and this means everything has to be earned. Progress that's given to you rather than earned isn't good progress for you. You avoid letting other people open doors for you because there's no learning opportunity in that. There's no real progress if there's no learning, and transforming your experience into learning is the whole point of being a human being.

Challenges, obstacles, and failures are a part of life. You're here to grow, learn, and improve. That's how God operates. God's not a slacker, and you don't have full partnership with God if you're a slacker.

Everything else fits.

Your seven other happiness capabilities, starting with individualism, all come together because of your permanent lifetime experience of an always-expanding transcendent relationship. Because of this eighth capability, everything else fits. Your growth in one area of capability reinforces your growth in all the others.

You have an individual relationship with God that leads to

uniqueness. America looks at itself as being established by the Creator. After all, the U.S. motto is, "In God we trust." There's the sense that there's an almost divine purpose to America.

Having lived outside of the U.S., I've noticed that there's a religious quality in America that isn't present in European countries. And in Canada, that quality of feeling connected and transcendent often comes from Canadians' relationship with nature.

People have said to me, "This relationship with God is something you've created in your imagination," but the fact is that I feel the relationship. People have also said, "What if you die and there's nothing after that?" and of course if that's the case, I won't care. It's a bet I'm willing to make.

Partnership beyond achievement.

You feel a growing certainty that your entire lifetime is in partnership with a higher sense of energy, order, and power. This partnership surpasses the events and achievements of daily practical life. You feel an ever-deepening happiness that expands outward into every area of your growth.

You don't get a report card. It's not as though a ledger is being kept. What it comes down to is, *to what degree did you maintain this connection in your life?*

The freedom to be yourself in America is a transcendent experience because you can make yourself into whomever you want and be the highest expression of yourself. And your partnership with a transcendent power gives you a greater sense of purpose.

UNIQUE RELATIONSHIP ...
WINNING
WINNING
WINNING
TRANSFORMATION
GROWTH
GROWTH
GROWTH
GROWTH
TEAMWORK
TEAMWORK
TEAMWORK
EXCEPTIONALISM
EXCEPTIONALISM
INGENUITY
INGENUITY
INGENUITY
INDIVIDUALISM

...LIFETIME PARTNERSHIP
SCEN-
NCE
WINNING
WINNING
WINNING
WINNING
TRANSFORMATION
TRANSFORMATION
GROWTH
GROWTH
GROWTH
GROWTH
TEAMWORK
TEAMWORK
TEAMWORK
TEAMWORK
EXCEPTIONALISM
EXCEPTIONALISM
EXCEPTIONALISM
INGENUITY
INGENUITY
INGENUITY
INDIVIDUALISM

Conclusion

Expansion Of Happiness

You permanently realize that pursuing happiness is not the goal or the result, but just the start of creating internal happiness and expanding it outward.

Over the course of your life, you've pursued many different things, hoping to achieve the happy state you thought was promised to you. And in America, you can do this pursuing in an unlimited number of ways. But all of this experience was just an opportunity to understand that happiness is actually the *start*—not the end.

American happiness is not a promise, but a bet made on you by a unique country: that you will make a uniquely permanent bet on yourself. Happiness in America starts when you first make the bet. It continually grows inside you as your lifetime bet grows through the eight happiness mindsets and then expands to help many other Americans to bet on themselves.

America wants you in the game. There's a lot of work you need to do, but you're equipped with the necessary mindsets, and if you ever fail, you'll get another chance.

The goal is inside.
You discover that being "American-minded"—understanding that a uniquely individual lifetime lies ahead of you—is your happiness starting point. With that realization of being a unique individual, you begin moving forward and upward, using the first American happiness mindset to master seven more.

People who turn to the government for their happiness will never be happy. They don't realize that it has to start with their own unique individuality. You have to take yourself seriously as an individual and bet on yourself just like the United States made a bet on you. Only then can you move on to the other seven mindsets, making sure that you'll be a happy American.

America's unlimited pursuits.

With the eight American happiness mindsets, you immediately begin doing things that are new and different. You think, say, and achieve in your own ingenious ways. What's exceptional about this is that no other country has ever wanted or planned for this to happen. You're very fortunate to get on this path early in life and make it your own.

There are unlimited paths you can take to pursue your happiness in the United States. All of the resources you need to be successful are out there, and what's required on your end is personal initiative and responsibility. You can't expect to be taken care of without recognizing what you uniquely have to offer.

Because it's based on your own individual definition of happiness, the path that's right for you isn't the path that's right for anyone else, so you have to find your unique path.

And happiness is only the beginning. Once you've found your happiness, you switch from *pursuing* it to *expanding* it.

Being uniquely you makes you happy.

American happiness is yours to grow by being yourself and then teaming up with others to grow the country. When the U.S. was established, the Founding Fathers bet that individual American citizens would bet on themselves and their futures. They bet that if they let everyone find their own happiness, they'd build a great country for everyone who lives in it.

Every individual starts by betting on themselves, developing themselves, and improving themselves. Your starting resource of individual happiness is multiplied by everyone else's in growing teamwork. And outside of your own teamwork projects, you know that countless others are doing the same thing.

America encourages innovation, which means there's room for each individual to find success and happiness, and there's no reason to be in competition with anyone else who's being uniquely themselves. In fact, by collaborating instead of competing with others who are focused on being useful, you can create something brand new and valuable.

Betting with the bettors.

As soon as you decided that being individually unique made you happy, you also became ingenious in creating new ways of expanding your happiness. You used your own uniqueness to bet on the uniqueness of other happy Americans who are betting on themselves. It endlessly expands.

It's all contained within a very deliberate, carefully constructed operating system that's structured to produce a particular type of outcome, but it allows for an amazing amount of variety, surprise, and unpredictability.

People who are attracted to the idea of betting on themselves will want to come to the United States if they aren't already residents because other countries don't let you make that bet.

Not all Americans have these mindsets. Not all Americans are happy. But the country has enough morale, momentum, and motivation that it can it can afford to have a portion of people who don't share these happiness mindsets. And if someone isn't happy, they can at least be pursuing happiness.

Your bet transcends your life.

The population of the United States has grown from about four million at the time the Constitution was signed to about 330 million, but everything an American needs today was put in place right at the beginning. It wasn't designed with any specific individual's happiness in mind, but rather for every single individual to be able to be happy by identifying and pursuing what that uniquely means for them.

Who you are is the starting point for being happy. You shouldn't try to be someone else, and you shouldn't compare yourself to other people. You have to take responsibility for your own happiness, choose to be happy right now, and make the decision to expand that happiness.

American happiness starts with your unique individualism, grows exceptionally bigger and better through transformative and winning teamwork, and then transcends everything that everyone created for themselves and others.

America's founders bet that this could happen. You're proving it was a good bet.

CREATING YOUR HAPPINESS...

...ENDLESSLY EXPANDING IT

The Strategic Coach Program

For Ambitious, Collaborative Entrepreneurs

You commit to growing upward through three transformative levels, giving yourself 25 years to exponentially improve every aspect of your work and life.

"American Happiness" is a crucial capability and a natural result of everything we coach in The Strategic Coach Program, a quarterly workshop experience for successful entrepreneurs who are committed and devoted to business and industry transformation for the long-term, for 25 years and beyond.

The Program has a destination for all participants—creating more and more of what we call "Free Zone Frontiers." This means taking advantage of your own unique capabilities, the unique capabilities around you, your unique opportunities, and your unique circumstances, and putting the emphasis on creating a life that is free of competition.

Most entrepreneurs grow up in a system where they think competition is the name of the game. The general way of looking at the world is that the natural state of affairs is competition, and collaboration is an anomaly.

Free Zone Frontier

The Free Zone Frontier is a whole new level of entrepreneurship that many people don't even know is possible. But once you start putting the framework in place, new possibilities open up for you. You create zones that are purely about collaboration. You start recognizing that collaboration is the natural state, and competition is the anomaly. It makes you look at things totally differently.

Strategic Coach has continually created concepts and thinking tools that allow entrepreneurs to more and more see their future in terms of Free Zones that have no competition.

Three levels of entrepreneurial growth.

Strategic Coach participants continually transform how they think, make decisions, communicate, and take action based on their use of dozens of unique entrepreneurial mindsets we've developed. The Program has been refined through decades of entrepreneurial testing and is the most concentrated, massive discovery process in the world created solely for transformative entrepreneurs who want to create new Free Zones.

Over the years, we've observed that our clients' development happens in levels of mastery. And so, we've organized the Program into three levels of participation, each of which involves two different types of transformation:

The Signature Level. The first level is devoted to your *personal* transformation, which has to do with how you're spending your time as an entrepreneur as well as how you're taking advantage of your personal freedom outside of business that your entrepreneurial success affords you. Focusing on improving yourself on a personal level before you move on to making significant changes in other aspects of your life and business is key because you have to simplify before you can multiply.

The second aspect of the Signature Level is how you look at your *teamwork*. This means seeing that your future consists of teamwork with others whose unique capabilities complement your own, leading to bigger and better goals that constantly get achieved at a measurably higher rate.

The 10x Ambition Level. Once you feel confident about your own personal transformation and have access to ever-expanding teamwork, you can think much bigger in terms of your *company*. An idea that at one time would have seemed scary and even impossible—growing your business 10x—is no longer a wild dream but a result of the systematic expansion of the teamwork model you've established. And because you're stable in the center, you won't get thrown off balance by exponential growth. Your life stays balanced and integrated even as things grow around you.

And that's when you're in a position to transform your relationship with your *market*. This is when your company has a huge impact on the marketplace that competitors can't even understand because they're not going through this transformative structure or thinking in terms of 25 years as you are. Thinking in terms of 25 years gives you an expansive sense of freedom and the ability to have big picture goals.

The Free Zone Frontier Level. Once you've mastered the first four areas of transformation, you're at the point where your company is self-managing and self-multiplying, which means that your time can now be totally freed up. At this stage, competitors become collaborators and it becomes all about your *industry*. You can consider everything you've created as a single capability you can now match up with another company's to create collaborations that go way beyond 10x.

And, finally, it becomes *global*. You immediately see that there are possibilities of going global—it's just a matter of combining your capabilities with those of others to create something exponentially bigger than you could ever have achieved on your own.

Global collaborative community.

Entrepreneurism can be a lonely activity. You have goals that the people you grew up with don't understand. Your family might not comprehend you at all and don't know why you keep wanting to expand, why you want to take new risks, why you want to jump to the next level. And so it becomes proportionately more important as you gain your own individual mastery that you're in a community of thousands of individuals who are on exactly the same journey.

In The Strategic Coach Program, you benefit from not only your own continual individual mastery but from the constant expansion of support from and collaboration with a growing global community of extraordinarily liberated entrepreneurs who will increasingly share with you their deep wisdom and creative breakthroughs as innovators in hundreds of different industries and markets.

If you've reached a jumping off point in your entrepreneurial career where you're beyond ready to multiply all of your capabilities and opportunities into a 10x more creative and productive formula that keeps getting simpler and more satisfying, we're ready for you.

For more information and to register for The Strategic Coach Program, call 416.531.7399 or 1.800.387.3206, or visit us online at *strategiccoach.com*.

THREE LEVELS OF FREE ZONE FRONTIER

FREE ZONE FRONTIER

- 100x Collaboration
- Perfect Fit VISION
- 25-Year Hero Target
- 100% Simplifier/Multiplier
- $15-Trillion Free Zone

10X AMBITION

- Self-Multiplying Company
- Simplifier/Multiplier
- Total Cash Confidence
- Always Be The Buyer
- The D.O.S. Conversation

SIGNATURE

- Self-Managing Company
- The Lifetime Extender
- Free, Focus, and Buffer Days
- Unique Ability Teamwork
- The Largest Cheque

FREE ZONE

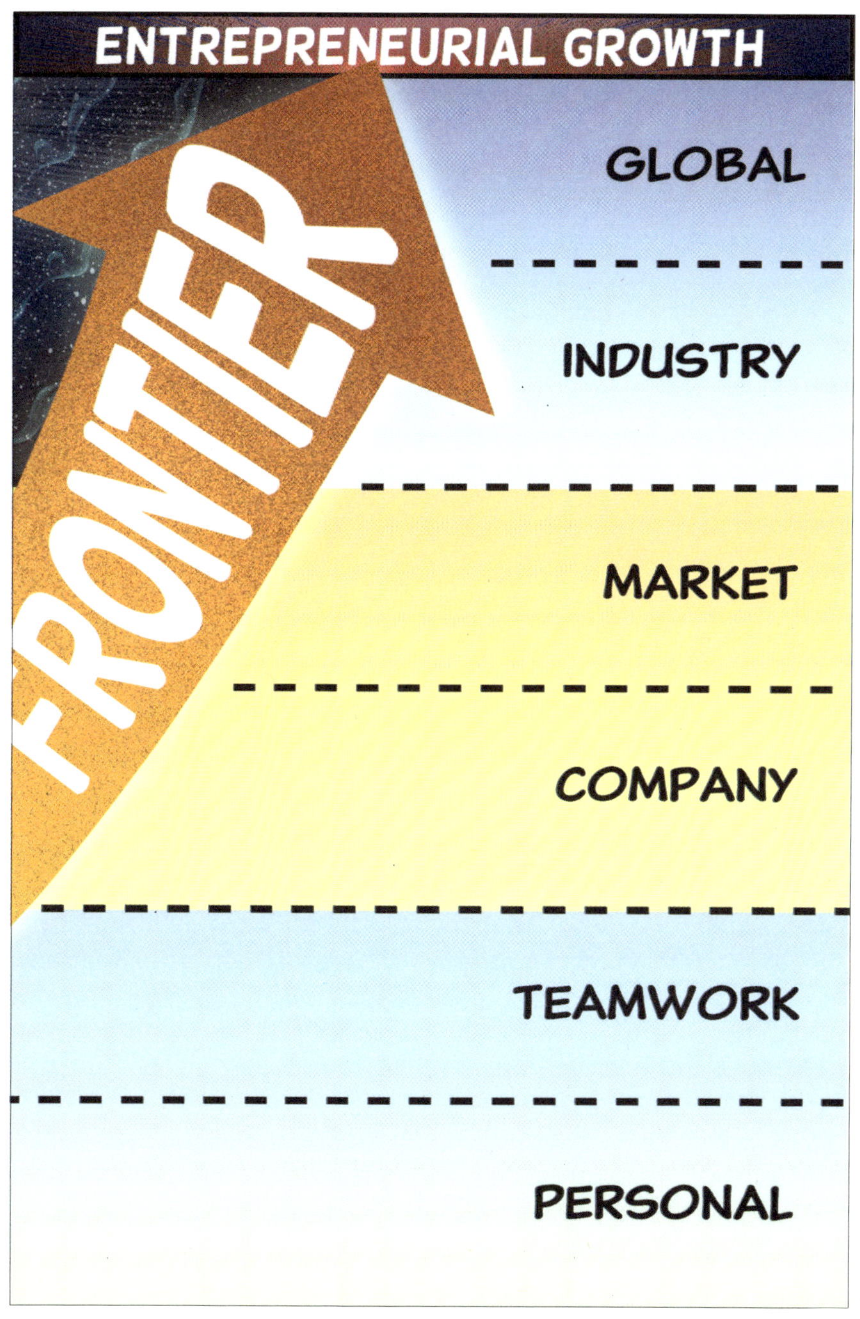
ENTREPRENEURIAL GROWTH
FRONTIER
GLOBAL
INDUSTRY
MARKET
COMPANY
TEAMWORK
PERSONAL

About The Authors

Dan Sullivan

Dan Sullivan is the founder and president of The Strategic Coach Inc. and creator of The Strategic Coach® Program, which helps accomplished entrepreneurs reach new heights of success and happiness. He is author of over 50 publications, including *The Great Crossover, The 21st Century Agent, Creative Destruction, How The Best Get Better*, and The Ambition Series of quarterly small books. He is co-author of *Who Not How, The Laws of Lifetime Growth*, and *The Advisor Century*.

Mark Young is a serial entrepreneur with current interests in advertising, real estate development, and media. He leveraged his education and passion for neuroscience, persuasion, NLP, and hypnosis to build Jekyll+Hyde Labs into one of the nation's most successful advertising agencies for challenger and emerging brand consumer products. Mark is also the managing partner of Two and Two Broadcasting, which provides content to radio stations across the country as well as podcast content. He is the co-host of the *American Checklist* podcast with Dan Sullivan.